D1486426

Paw Prints

Beagles

by Kaitlyn Duling

Ideas for Parents and Teachers

Bullfrog Books let children practice reading informational text at the earliest reading levels. Repetition, familiar words, and photo labels support early readers.

Before Reading

- Discuss the cover photo. What does it tell them?
- Look at the picture glossary together. Read and discuss the words.

Read the Book

- "Walk" through the book and look at the photos. Let the child ask questions. Point out the photo labels.
- Read the book to the child, or have him or her read independently.

After Reading

- Prompt the child to think more. Ask: Have you ever seen a beagle? Would you like to play with one?

Bullfrog Books are published by Jump!
5357 Penn Avenue South
Minneapolis, MN 55419
www.jumplibrary.com

Library of Congress Cataloging-in-Publication Data

Names: Duling, Kaitlyn, author.
Title: Beagles / by Kaitlyn Duling.
Description: Minneapolis, MN : Jump!, 2018.
Series: Paw prints
Series: Bullfrog books | Includes index.
Audience: Ages 5 to 8. | Audience: Grades K to 3.
Identifiers: LCCN 2017039652 (print)
LCCN 2017043174 (ebook)
ISBN 9781624967658 (ebook)
ISBN 9781624967641 (hardcover : alk. paper)
Subjects: LCSH: Beagle (Dog breed)—Juvenile literature.
Classification: LCC SF429.B3 (ebook)
LCC SF429.B3 D85 2018 (print) | DDC 636.753/7—dc23
LC record available at https://lccn.loc.gov/2017039652

Editor: Jenna Trnka
Book Designer: Molly Ballanger

Photo Credits: Antonov Roman/Shutterstock, cover; Svetography/Shutterstock, 1; Eric Isselee/Shutterstock, 3, 24; GROSSEMY VANESSA/Alamy, 4, 23br; Lenkadan/Shutterstock, 5, 23tr; David Harrigan/Getty, 6–7; De Agostini/Biblioetca Ambrosiana/Getty, 8–9, 23tl; Olga Kuzyk/Shutterstock, 10, 23ml; ARTSILENSE/Shutterstock, 11; Alexey Androsov/Shutterstock, 12–13; Minden Pictures/SuperStock, 14–15, 23mr; Vivienstock/Shutterstock, 16; Aneta Jungerova/Shutterstock, 17; Be Good/Shutterstock, 18–19; Nina Buday/Shutterstock, 20–21; Akitamedles/Shutterstock, 22; Rainer Lesniewski/Shutterstock, 23bl.

Printed in the United States of America at Corporate Graphics in North Mankato, Minnesota.

Table of Contents

The Nose Knows

Look, a beagle!

His nose is
to the ground.

Why?
He smells something!
Let's follow him!

A beagle follows its nose.
This dog has a great
sense of smell.

nose

7

Beagles are hounds.
They are from England.
They were bred to hunt.

This beagle has black on its coat.

coat

This one is just
tan and white.

ear

The ears flop down.
The coat is short.

A beagle is small.
But it is loud.
It howls.

His tail stands up.
He is on the hunt!

16

A beagle will run far.

He follows the scent.

17

Beagles love to run.

They love to play, too.

Beagles love friends.

Do you want a beagle
for a friend?

A Beagle Up Close

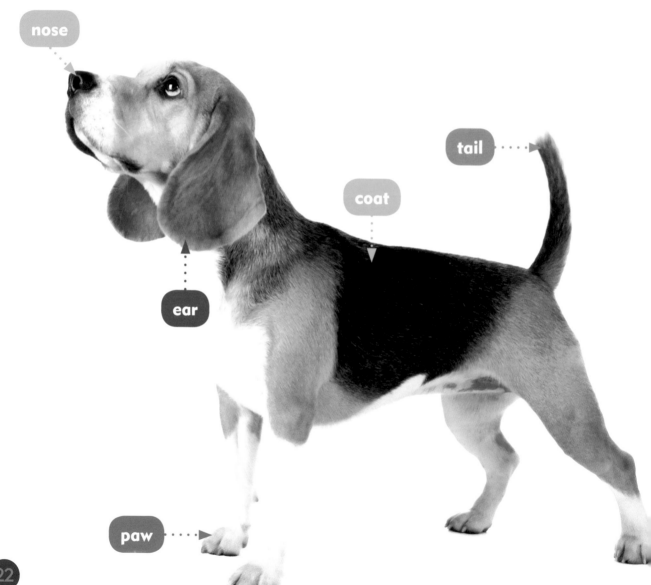

Picture Glossary

bred
Developed as a dog breed.

hounds
Dogs that are used for hunting and can track by scent.

coat
A dog's fur.

howls
Makes a long, loud sound.

England
A large country in the United Kingdom.

scent
A smell.

Index

To Learn More

Learning more is as easy as 1, 2, 3.

1) Go to www.factsurfer.com

2) Enter "beagles" into the search box.

3) Click the "Surf" button to see a list of websites.

With factsurfer.com, finding more information is just a click away.